The Storm Continues...

Gleaning from the Calm, Storm, and Aftermath of a marriage when the forecast was for sunshine and clear skies!

by

Stacy L. Cobbins

The Storm Continues...

Please e-mail Stacyc2cs@gmail.com to inquire about becoming a life coaching client of Stacy Cobbins Consulting and Coaching, LLC and to share your life stories and questions that Stacy may address in her videos.

Stacy L. Cobbins

Presented to

By

Date

Copyright ©2021 Stacy L. Cobbins

All rights reserved. No part of this publication may be reproduced, distributed, or transmitted in any form or by any means, including photocopying, recording, or other electronic or mechanical methods, without the prior written permission of the publisher, except in the case of brief quotations embodied in critical reviews and certain other noncommercial uses permitted by copyright law.

ISBN-978-1-951300-13-5

Liberation's Publishing – West Point - Mississippi

The Storm Continues...

Gleaning from the Calm, Storm, and Aftermath of a marriage when the forecast was for sunshine and clear skies!

Dedication

To my child, you know my heart beats at the will of pleasing God and being your example of a good Christian woman. I am reminded God answers prayers and takes care of His each time I see you. I love you and want you to always know this and to please Him!

To my parents, sister, and brother, thank you for everything and allowing me to be the middle child I am.

To my mentor, thank you for your leadership, critiques, and everything to help me soar as a woman and professional beneath your wings.

To my former "Act Like a Virtuous Lady, Think Like the Spiritual Man" teen girls, thank you for using my real-life story and biblical teachings to build upon your Christian foundation for times of testing and storms.

Stacy L. Cobbins

Table of Content

Foreword 11

The Calm or Light Before the Storm 13

   Perception of Being on Top – Marriage, Motherhood, Business, Roles in the Church 13

   Signs the Sun is Going Down Before the Storm 19

   Tornado Watch 23

      White Lies – Funds, Church Engagements, Trips, Employee Relationships 23

   Tornado Warning 33

      Pushed to Develop a Hobby and Separate Means to Generate Income 33

      Response Received After the Doctor's News 36

In the Storm 43

   The Tornado Hits 43

      Required Partial Hysterectomy 43

      Life Threatening Infection Shone Light on Kidney Mass and Liver Lesions 45

      Discovery of Yet Another Extra Marital Affair with an Employee in Our Family Business 51

Coming Out of The Storm 60

   The Aftermath 60

   The Façade to the Church 61

   The Façade to the Family 62

   The Half-Hearted Attempt to Savage the Marriage 68

Quest for a New Employer 77
The Divorce Filing 81
Assessing the Damage 88
   Divorce Cares Support Group 88
   Health Issues Resurface 89
   Effect on the Child 90
   The Family's Response 92
   The Church's Response 94
   The Staff in The Family Dental Practice's Response 97
   Counseling 98
   Spiritual Leader 100
The Road to Recovery/Rebuilding 101
   Divorce Awarded 102
   Acknowledge the Disappointment and Grieve the Process
   103
   Healing 103
   Trusting God 104

The Storm Continues 106

The Storm Cycle Continues – Headed to A Storm, In A Storm, Coming Out of A Storm 106
   Calm 106
   In the Storm 106
   Coming Out of the Storm 109

The Storm Continues...

Foreword

Young and seasoned ladies and gentleman know your worth without a woman or man (boyfriend or husband or girlfriend or wife.) Feel valuable in the absence of a mate. This is different from being arrogant. Self-worth allows you to feel good single and as added value when an opportunity arises to be in a committed relationship that is expected to lead to marriage as well as in marriage.

Storms are preceded by red flags. Don't ignore them especially after a suspected red flag is confirmed. The second a red flag or deal breaker is confirmed please R-U-N!

Remaining in a toxic situation, lowers your value, enables a mate to disrespect you, and delays the one God has for you. The Bible says all things work together for the good of them who love The Lord and are the called according to His purpose. God's purpose is to prosper you, keep you in good health, and give you an expected end. He is able to do that! Will you trust Him? It won't be easy, but you'll get through it.

The Storm Continues...

As you read the upcoming pages, allow my real-life experience and tips from The Storm Continues ... to help identify traits from your relationships that may be affecting your value. After each main section, there is a Notes page. Take the time to assess a current relationship or process what happened in a previous relationship as it relates to the applicable phase of the storm that you would have just read. I pray that in each phase of The Storm Continues… you'll recall things from your own story and make the decision to value yourself as you read my story.

During this time, life and marriage appeared as living the American Dream.

The Calm or Light Before the Storm

Perception of Being on Top - Marriage, Motherhood, Business, Roles in the Church

Ah, can you imagine having previously had sunny days, mansions, dream vacations, five luxury vehicles, and fourteen other vehicles (inclusive of an antique truck?) Imagine being at the top in your career and business, fulfilling leadership roles in professional networks, enjoying motherhood, being called Sister (<u>Insert Your Marital Last Name</u>) in the Christian community. Imagine being an active usher, Sunday School teacher, teen girls' ministry leader, and coordinator for a group of widows at your local church while being in a marriage to the man with whom you planned to be married to forever?

Imagine loving this same man who you've experienced all of these things with for over half of your life. Your marital relationship would have started five months after graduating with your bachelor's degree and while serving a total of eight years in the United States Army Reserves. Can you add to that imagination the lack of knowledge of your man's interest in becoming a dentist and the calling from God for him to preach and teach the <u>Bible?</u> If you can't imagine being this woman, that's okay. I'm about to tell you the real-life story of her.

I am that woman. Google my name, Stacy L. Cobbins, for a picture of me. I am the female who used to live this life. Etch a picture in your brain of my young, twenty-three-year-old, tall, thin frame, with long so-called good hair, caramel complexion, and a pretty smile (but crooked teeth and an overbite,) dressed conservatively. Take a journey with me, the middle child of three, while I give you a face-to-face encounter with one of my life's storms.

Yes, you might say, "So what! Everyone has or will go through a storm. Nobody's perfect. You win some. You lose some. That's just life!"

> Everyone has or will go through a storm.

My response will be, "It's my storm and I am telling it in hopes of helping someone. If you haven't gone through it, this might help you prepare or assess if you're headed straight to it."

Here's a part of my true story that may help you to decide if you are at a similar phase of preparing your emergency preparedness kit for a storm. Put in your mind this Stacy who never wanted children finding herself with a tubal pregnancy four years into her twenty-five years and ten months marriage. How did she end up trying to have a child after previously not wanting one?

This quest was incited by a tubal pregnancy and a husband who knew before our marriage that I did not want children. Yet, he continued to express a desire for eight children! He was my college sweetheart. He was the guy with pretty eyes, in a popular fraternity, and in a pretty good ride. I chose to overlook the fact that he was shorter than I am. Most remarkable was he chose me, the college girl who drove the Cavalier Z24 with the personalized tag that read "To Kute" because TooCute was taken. Out of all the pretty girls at the University, he asked me over the radio, "Would you

> Out of all the pretty girls at the University, he asked me over the radio, "Would you marry me?"

marry me" for the entire Golden Triangle Area to hear. Ayeeee, ayeeee! You may think I should have felt like his prize and very lucky. Wrong! Let me prepare you for this storm that hit me, Stacy L. Cobbins.

There is a probability that you like most of the traits I used to describe this shorter man. The most exciting part of a relationship is when it first begins. You may overlook things you thought you wouldn't before. You must be able to distinguish when it is or is not okay to overlook the differences you and your mate have. The thrill of the new relationship, a person's popularity, material things, and good looks may make a forecast for sunshine and clear skies. But the ratio of females to a male can bolster a player and ladies' man mentality in the best of men. And, it can yield a saditty woman.

> You must be able to distinguish when it is or is not okay to overlook the differences you and your mate have.

We were in the tenth year of marriage and living in the second home we had built. It was our first mansion. This was after having lived in four apartments and to then live in our third house.

After a tubal pregnancy at year four and enduring a pregnancy that consisted of five long months of bed rest in year ten, the weather forecast for the day was 100% sunshine with some cloud cover. It was the blessing of a fulfilled quest, a safe birth of our healthy eight-pound baby boy. He was born at a quarter to one in the afternoon on January 28, 2004, three weeks before his due date.

What a welcomed weather change from the cloudy weather the preceding days. This good weather made it easier to suppress the powerful female intuition of an in-the-closet cheating spouse's return home from another twelve hours of hunting (or so the time was disguised.) Instantly, our happy family didn't feel like a façade. We parents and our newborn, all wearing Mississippi State University's attire, looked like the picture-perfect family. That is because we were the proud parents of a new baby. We enhanced the look of perfection by adding pictures of our baby with both sets of grandparents dressed in our undergraduate university paraphernalia. That alma mater is where our dating relationship began.

Are you visualizing this correctly? Surely, you see Mrs. Perfect now, holding one of eight children for her wonderful, well-respected husband now known as the dentist and businessman. Our three-member family was living in our first mansion, an approximate five-thousand square-foot home that we had built on acreage with a pond in a neighborhood that became a gated community. I hear you cheering and applauding. Yesss, hunty look at the young, black, successful couple who are living the American Dream.

Back to my slick hunting comment made above, it should be easy to see how at this point I was made to feel I should be grateful to have a good and hardworking husband who had acceptable hobbies. I knew and was told there are a lot of wives who wished when their husband was not at work that he'd not stay out all night and away from home or lost the money needed to cover the bills.

It is easy to be on the outside looking in. A female reader may consider gambling, drinking, or not working a worse activity for her fiancé or husband to do or as a substitute for my husband's activities. Stop and think. What red flags are waving as warnings that are being overlooked and ignored in your relationship?

> It is easy to be on the outside looking in.

My red flags were camouflaged as time away for patient emergencies, hunting, fishing, preaching, business trips, and getaways with friends. With the expansion of our family, we appeared picture perfect and brightened sun rays. Darkness had to precede the change in weather headed our way.

Signs the Sun is Going Down Before the Storm

I and our newborn son were insufficient to sustain the sunlight. We couldn't keep the head of our house home. The red flag present during dating, signaling other women, reared its head after we wedded. Young and old ladies from all walks of life were willing and waiting with open legs, arms, and mouths.

The job I achieved at the top of my profession in my early thirties became a gamble. I had to pick it or my baby. Considering this child was born after nearly eleven years of marriage and who experienced health challenges from asthma and many allergies, the decision was tilted.

There were episodes of family members keeping our son in our home. Various nannies never passed trial runs of my unreasonable list of expectations. Therefore, I left a dream job at the top of my profession. But I never stopped performing and managing multiple functions in our family's dental practice for which I was instrumental in establishing.

Early on, we both knew cheating ran on both sides of our family. Unlike him, the buck stopped with me. More than once, he told me that at least he didn't stay out overnight or have outside children. (Whelp, you'll have to read other chapters to see if he spoke too soon.)

Are you still envisioning my picture? Are you seeing the strong, no-nonsense, got it all together, and in control woman? Does it look like she's about to describe a storm where the eye of it includes her good, well-respected husband who had become a preacher after her first born? So how could there be truth to nonsense in a marriage when things and both parties looked like they have it ALL together? Remember, the name you googled and picture you saw is of me. I am the lady who earned an advanced degree from Vanderbilt University, multiple certifications, good paying jobs, credited by lawyers in their publications, and had a perfect family who owned businesses. I was married to a king, short in stature but mighty in houses, land, cars, businesses, and religious teachings. It's the picture of the perfect me you see with an excellent mate.

Fear, doubt, and insecurity were not returned from your Google search nor did you see any on Stacy L. Cobbins. You sat beside and saw me working in the church. You enjoyed all of my over-the-top parties and saw me as happy as I could be, right? Psyche! Yeah, I was the quiet and sometimes shy one who that pretty eyed preacher referenced and honored from the stage or pulpit as his beautiful wife and the one who managed the businesses. Are you still having trouble recognizing me? Stop, put things aside, and remember who the tall, cute lady was always in a different (sometimes name brand) outfit, possessed the latest electronic gadget, already been to that vacation destination, who rode in a different Mercedes, and lived in a bigger home with more amenities before you could remember the address of her previous one.

Yeah, you saw me in the bright sunlight and probably a place people have or are viewing you. Remember you're reading about the lady who was headed to The Storm during the period in this book considered the Light or Calm Before the Storm.

The Storm Continues...

In summary, in the calm or light before the storm is the point where others on the outside looking in wish they could be. They want to trade their lives to experience how living your "best life" can be. WARNING: Looks can be deceiving.

> **WARNING:** Looks can be deceiving.

Tornado Watch

White Lies – Funds, Church Engagements, Trips, Employee Relationships

For those on the outside looking in at me, you did not know a Tornado Watch had already been issued. That's because the Calm or Light before the storm was transcending darkness. What darkness you say? Honey Chile, you didn't see it? You didn't hear it? Deep down in your knower, you didn't know it. Let me tell you. That's because darkness is intangible. You cannot pick that beast up and touch it, overthrow it, or stop it. The need to issue a Tornado Watch starts before the meteorologist sees the favorable conditions.

> That's because darkness is intangible. You cannot pick that beast up and touch it, overthrow it, or stop it.

My conditions for this storm that was brewing consisted of invisible seeds that were fertilized and watered. This required an alert of a Tornado Watch. In the watch were unmet wants and needs, negative childhood experiences and memories, outsiders, and ultimately lies and deceit.

When you are in a relationship with a man with the wrong motives or who possesses a short man syndrome, you must be free of insecurity, low self-esteem, and fear. Otherwise, you are licensing him to further engage in control, deceit, and manipulation. Let me give you an example.

I am a product of adultery. Most of my childhood, the children would talk about me for the decisions and actions of others out of my control. Likewise, I made plenty of my own bad childhood decisions. My and others' decisions from my childhood are things of the past. But, for some reason, I allowed people's thoughts and opinions to impact me and plant a seed of insecurity.

Even near my wedding day, it got back to me that a relative said my marriage was not going to last after my husband completed his dental degree. Then, there were others who said as much education as he gets, you be sure to get just as much. You don't want to be where you have given him your whole life, and he leaves you.

All of those things played in my head. Two months after we got married, I discovered a white lie (red flag) that dealt with funds. I immediately recalled thoughts of the things mentioned previously and jumped into survival mode stemming from fear and insecurity. Guess what? He knew this and increased manipulation and deception.

I thought back to when we first started dating, he would take me shopping to the mall and trips out-of-town. I thought that showed me I was special, cared for, and loved a way no other had shown me. I didn't know it was a manipulation strategy that increased my dependence and insecurity and ultimately his control for me to feel better off with him.

Have you ever compared Who Was your no more to Who Is? If so, you may have thought, ok I am better off with Who Is. You probably fantasized, if I stay with Who Is, I can get xyz, eat at xyz, or go to xyz! Or, worse yet, you may be now counting on your training Who Is to do (or not do) whatever the red flag is that tells you to run immediately!

You probably fantasized, if I stay with Who Is, I can get xyz, eat at xyz, or go to xyz!

The Storm Continues...

One of the biggest and most noticeable white lies (red flags) I was told at the beginning of marriage was that a dental classmate, who had become a friend, allowed my husband to use his boat whenever he wanted to. Lo and behold, the friend's boat actually was owned by my husband. But it was parked at the friend's house because we didn't live in a place appropriate for a boat's storage.

In the second decade of our marriage and while living in our second mansion in a gated community, I was told another lie involving the same friend. I was told the friend's daughter was getting married and wanted my husband to officiate the wedding in Florida. The date was the same *Saturday* in July as our son's filmmaker's workshop film debut. As if being considerate and to fulfill the officiant obligation, my husband said he would make the trip alone. This meant our son and I couldn't accompany the head of our house to Florida for the friend's daughter's wedding. Guess what? The wedding was on a Sunday. Someone else officiated, not my husband. That was an opportunity my husband embellished and took to take a mistress, who knew he was married and a preacher, on a trip for sex on the beach, not the drink.

Then, there are the lies that my husband told me that involved business funds. He would request that I produce meal and incidental payments for employees' simultaneous business travel. Yet, he would use additional business and other funds to wine, dine, and seduce certain ones.

I can't forget the midweek engagements for churches which this same wonderful husband was invited. Even when he had hopes of pastoring, he'd find value in going to various churches without his family. Such church engagements seem to be accepted and mysteriously attended when he started slacking in attendance at our church's Wednesday night Bible Study.

There were also strange things that would abruptly interrupt his presence or lead to his absence during our church services. Once during a one-week church conference, he had to leave early. We had driven separately. He texted once he was outside of the church to say he was leaving to go help a friend in the clergy with a truck that allegedly broke down. NOTE: The clergy friend had lots of local relatives not in the midst of a church service wearing a suit. Plus, the truck supposedly broke down frequently. During that same week, another time he was a no-show to church for helping the same friend for the same reason.

After I left the corporate world and public sector employment, for many years I operated and managed our private businesses without other employment. This was another ingredient that fed my insecurity, his control, and support for a Tornado Alert. Our joint efforts in the family business gave him the ability to make me lose the seed of control he verbalized that I had. However, this was clearly inaccurate when it came to discharging employees for which there was indication of an inappropriate relationship. It was his words that nothing was there or going on with the employees. You and I make a good team. He would tell me he loved me and poured on gifts like expensive vehicles supportive of lavish living that made his plan of manipulation, deceit, and control successful.

Be alert to these ingredients for they make conditions favorable to issue a Tornado Alert. Ladies, I warn you. Know your worth.

Know your worth. Ask yourself, "have I been or am I being bought?

Ask yourself, "have I been or am I being bought? If every time you have a valid or deal breaker reason to leave, you feel like you can't eat at the fancy restaurant, wear the designer clothes, drive the fancy cars, or live like the queen Hollywood has led you to believe, you are likely being controlled and bought by a master manipulator and deceiver.

Some will read this and think or say, as long as he is paying the bills and providing that kind of life for me, girllll! You should be happy. No, trust me. All of that is vanity and it's false and temporary happiness. Real talk, when there is a tornado watch, don't just see the signs and not check your emergency kit. You must hunker down and prepare just in case the Tornado Watch turns into a Tornado Warning.

Now, I must remind you again. This book is from my view. And, at the time of my writing this, I have already lived these moments. So, the perspectives I have provided for this Tornado Watch portion of the book are After Actions Reviews. In other words, I had no clue my conditions, including those described earlier in this chapter, were representative of a Tornado Watch. In fact, I thought I was doing well. I had beaten the odds of becoming a teenage mother; I had not become pregnant before I was married; and my husband hadn't left me after graduating dental school. Not only had I graduated high school, I graduated from two different universities with a bachelor's and a double concentration major master's degree. This had not been achieved before on my side of the family.

The thought, without the proof, of a cheating husband was better than what women on both sides of our family had survived and were enduring. After the Tornado Watch was obvious, I had also earned two certifications, achieved a Director level position, and became a business owner in a marriage that I knew had glitches but nothing to prevent it from everlasting.

After the fact, I wonder was I crazy? The signs were there as early as dating. In fact, the marriage proposal over the radio really resulted because he saw someone else had an interest in me. See, we had broken up about yet another white lie (red flag) that ladies' man was good for telling. This time, in our courtship, there was a party he hosted but lied and

> The signs were there as early as dating.

said his college co-workers were having it for employees only.

Five months later, on our wedding day, a message left on our answering machine revealed another lie. He had been absent from work the entire week of our wedding. His coworker's voice message said he picked up my soon to be husband's check for him, since he was off all week getting ready for our wedding. This message contradicted the story my soon to be husband had me believing prior to hearing the message on the answering machine. He clearly stated he could not take off the week of our wedding because he had to work. He was not off helping with the wedding nor was he working! If it was necessary to tell work and me a lie, there must have been some hanky panky business going on!

We talked over the phone on the wedding about the message. I told my fiancé if all of the guests had not come for the wedding there would not be a wedding that day, May 28, 1994. See God had given me a way of escape on my wedding day that I did not take. Pride stood up because of all of the money that had been spent and how things would look. Pride was the reason I said yes to the proposal over the radio. Like the wedding day, the grand proposal and wedding day took place right after big lies (red flags) were uncovered.

Be quiet everyone, please. I can hear ya through these pages saying, "she knew she was about to marry a liar and a cheat. She should stop pretending. Well, keep reading.

Did you notice something? We were shacking up prior to getting married. We both had just graduated with our undergraduate degrees in December of 1993. After accepting his Christmas Day over the radio marriage proposal, I relocated for a new job that started right after the holidays. He moved in with me. We were young, dumb, and engaged to be married. Therefore, living together before getting married was viewed as ok. Plus, our wedding was five months away and he would give me the security I needed to live unafraid in a new place. We both believed in God and "went to church." (If you too hope to get married or are engaged to be married, know that I am not condoning what we did. God's will is for us to abstain from sex before marriage. When we disobey God, we operate outside of His will. Disobedience alone ushers in storms.)

Tornado Warning

Pushed to Develop a Hobby and Separate Means to Generate Income

Can you hear it? Turn down the radio and the TV. Do I hear sirens sounding? Noooo, wait a minute. That is not the police or an ambulance I am hearing. That's the weather siren going off to warn me the weather conditions are serious.

If you are a reader who lives or has lived in Mississippi in the spring or fall, you know very well what I am describing. Unlike rainy weather with thunderstorms and lightning, a Tornado Warning affects the mind very differently. Just the memory of a Tornado's destruction to the strongest building, a deep-rooted tree, and the loss of lives makes the average person heed a tornado warning. Guess what! I ignored this Tornado Warning. I didn't prepare nor did I take cover!

Years later after the family dental business, the cash cow, was in a new location that was being purchased, growth was visible. I had become accustomed to working nights and weekends remotely, in addition to working on-site during the day to maintain my role in our multiple businesses.

I did all of that and balanced the needs of my husband, our son, home, and church. It didn't seem odd that my husband encouraged me to reduce my in-office work hours and take as much time away from the actual site as I needed. In fact, I thought that spoke positively. The policies and procedures I had created made for smooth business operations. Several systems, processes, and vendors I initiated are still in place in the dental practice that remains in operations today.

During this phase, we employed a couple of clinical professionals and multiple entry level employees. Multiple times before I had proof, my intuition would signal there was something not quite right. Female-after-female employee would always seem to be in his office. The excuses told to me about matters they were addressing were out of my accounting, administrative, or HR purview. The Employee Handbook became a book of jokes. He picked and chose what would be supported inconsistently, depending upon the threat or level of relationship with the employee. Later I would receive a resignation for those with whom an inappropriate relationship was suspected. It's my belief our boss was just good with manipulation and deception tactics. In order for anyone to be terminated, there had to be an overwhelming performance deficiency. Once, one former employee came by for a visit while I was in the office. She poked her head in to speak to me, the wife and one in the business she hated. My husband and boss followed up after she left and said the former employee had come by seeking ortho services and to be reemployed. Then, he went on to say (with a smile on his face) that he didn't take the bait because he knew it was more that the young lady was seeking.

Instead of the first mistress employee being a lesson for the businessman and member of the clergy, he never would repent. He became bolder, more comfortable, and resilient with the next newbie. Each episode, I left and worked outside of the business. Sometimes we would get counseling. This would be followed by his expressions of love and need. Then, he'd come up with something that appeared as if he was looking out for me. And, of course, I'd get a just because (better known as guilt) expensive gift. He would say there was nothing between him and the employee. The best manipulation strategy he enacted was that I needed an outlet instead of always working to care for our son, home, church, and marital duties. He knew I could and loved to cook. I credit him with finding and getting me started with a cake decorating hobby. That hobby, turned non-profit charity, took some time away from me being in the office during the day.

Response Received After the Doctor's News

Yes, that really was the siren indicating a Tornado Warning. This means that not only are conditions favorable, but an actual tornado has been spotted and approaching the area. In the previous section, I heard the sound. I heard the sound alerting me that a tornado was headed my way. And, like you, I had to turn on the news and check my cell phone to make sure the sound I was hearing was true.

It was 2017 when heavy and long-lasting menstrual cycles were taking over the life I was leading. I had prior surgeries to remove fibroid tumors. Those things returned more than one time but this time they returned with a vengeance. My cycles were so heavy that it was nothing for me to awaken and see I bled excessively and onto my bedsheets. I could be walking, minding my own business, and experience my menstrual cycle gush out and show through my clothes. I could not befriend white clothes because my menstrual cycle would embarrass me and show up before it was scheduled. Frequently, I became sick and remained in bed from its extensive, long lasting, and monthly pain.

The description above may have seen too detailed, long, and drawn out. I just want you to have a clear picture of what I experienced most months for two weeks.

The following words are what the doctor used to report the tornado in my area: Hi Stacy. So, you're still having the same complaints about your cycle. The medicine is not working. Let me do a quick exam. Look, at your age, 46, the likelihood of conceiving another child and one without health issues is a very low percent. I want to give you some brochures for you to consider some options. I think we have tried everything we can including medicine. I recommend a hysterectomy. It depends on what all is involved once we start as far as the type necessary. Generally, unless there is something major, we will avoid a big cut by doing it laparoscopically. If you agree to it, we can do a partial hysterectomy which will leave your ovaries intact. Or, we can do a full hysterectomy where your uterus and ovaries are removed also. An additional thing for you to know about a full hysterectomy, since you are not at the age of menopause, is that it will put you in immediate menopause. You will need a hormone supplement to replace the hormones your body will no longer produce.

For someone like me at my age and on top in my life after having suffered with menstrual cycles as long as I can remember, I bet you thought I was jumping for joy after receiving my doctor's news. By now, you know I'd had a child. If I went with a hysterectomy option, as a married woman, I could make love to my husband without the breaks my long menstrual cycles required me. And, hip, hip, hooray, I could wear white and pack whatever kinds of clothes I wanted for trips.

Those exciting thoughts were short lived. I conveyed the information from the doctor to my cheating spouse. Instead of him showing compassion, concern, and care that I may be relieved of the painful month-after-month long menstrual cycle, his livid and selfish words were felt like the impact of a Tornado's hit. Those hurtful words included, "So that means I can't have NO MORE children? I might not have grandchildren! Are you kidding me? So, I guess you have to do what's best for you?!"

Crushed, I spoke hurtful words back to him. "You must be crazy. We are too old for children anyway. We have classmates with grandchildren. We already experienced having our son in our thirties. And, his classmates have asked him if we were his parents or grandparents. Man, please! If we haven't been successful in but once out of three pregnancies, it's not meant to be!"

He told me there was nothing wrong with him. And, that I knew he wanted to have lots of children.

I said, so are you saying something is wrong with me. I have been pregnant three times and am thankful for having one child successfully. It could be that you are the problem. You only have one sibling who has more than one child just like me! You knew I didn't want any children when we got married. You can go out and get you more children. But don't expect to do like you do with our one child and leave all the responsibility to me to keep me tied down. You go about life living footloose and fancy free. All you want is the image of a preacher with his quiver full. You don't want the responsibility. You don't give enough time to our existing family.

Hear me people! Neither the woman nor the man can change the other. It's only the grace of God who can soften hearts. Your job is to hear a person's heart and heed the warnings. I and my husband advised each other about our wishes for a family before marriage. Yes, there were some childhood experiences and hurts that played into my initial thoughts of not wanting children. Likewise, there were some childhood experiences that played into the desires of my husband for children. Do not start a marriage with a plan that either spouse's desires will change. In a lot of situations, wants and needs can and do change. You read earlier how the mere tubal pregnancy led to my quest to have children. Even at the age of 46, I had not closed the door to having more than the one I have. In situations like this, the test will come. And, the result will reveal hidden resentment, unforgotten comments, and/or adulterous activities.

> Neither the woman nor the man can change the other. It's only the grace of God who can soften hearts.

Another thing, in heated conversations refrain

from giving your spouse a hall pass to go outside your marriage. You read correctly. I told my husband, the one I knew to be a cheater, to go out and get more children. That was not what I meant! And, I certainly didn't want him to do it by committing more adultery. Why would a wife say that? Why did Sarah say that? Was that a sign of insecurity or low self-value? It certainly was not an act of obedience to God.

NOTES

What Have or Are You Gleaning from Your Current or Previous Relationship "Headed to The Storm?"

In the Storm

Just like a weather storm, this life storm hit more than one area quickly.

The Tornado Hits

Required Partial Hysterectomy

After the warning was proven to be correct for my area of life, the initial impact following the loud Tornado Warning was the hit to my life caused by my husband's response to me about the doctor's news. He became more withdrawn with our three-member family and within our home. Simply put, he was doing more of his own thing. This didn't mean he wasn't still good at window dressing for the church and both sides of our families. But, behind the scenes, just like I knew when he was cheating, there were always excuses (lies given as reasons told for the truth.) The most popular reason he would give for his absence with our three-member family and in our home covered his time away. He would say that it took longer to perform dental procedures and surgeries in the various places, organizations' meetings required his attendance, or some happenings that supported his need to travel separately to church or to visit my family.)

To cover the damage from the tornado's hit, I

beefed up my efforts to build relationships with those started at the church and a Wives w/Lives group. I was trying to fill the void I felt from the damage my marriage sustained.

I made the decision to go ahead with the hysterectomy. Yes, I prayed before I made the big decision. In my private conversation with God, I wanted to know the decision He wanted me to make. I prayed, "God even at my age You are able to work miracles. If it is Your will for me not to have a hysterectomy, then let me miss my next cycle and have a positive pregnancy test. This way I will know without a doubt not to go through with a hysterectomy."

Before my next cycle was due, it came and with a vengeance. I was sad and simultaneously thankful. God didn't make me wait for His decision. I had no reason to have false hope. I accepted God's will was for me to have the hysterectomy.

On Monday, August 28, 2017, I was admitted for surgery. The doctor spoke with my husband and they chose a partial hysterectomy versus a full hysterectomy. This was because the doctor told my husband that he would receive the brunt ☺ of the mood swings that would follow surgery because I would be in immediate menopause.

In the midst of the surgery, unbeknownst to me until afterwards, the doctor spoke with my husband again. This time it was for permission to have a surgeon to perform a Hernia repair. There was a nice size hernia beneath my navel. Permission was granted and the hernia repair surgery took place.

Life Threatening Infection Shone Light on Kidney Mass and Liver Lesions

Almost immediately after I was discharged from the hospital following my hysterectomy and hernia repair, I became sick. I would call the doctors' offices and they would say the various things I was experiencing was normal and to call back if I spiked a fever. I couldn't eat or drink or hold anything down. It was excruciatingly painful to urinate or have a bowel movement. And, unlike the proud supporters of females who benefitted from having a hysterectomy before, I was still experiencing vaginal bleeding.

Before the weekend following the surgery concluded, I was in the emergency room. I was traumatized and thought I was going to die. My mother had come down the Sunday morning to see me for herself because her motherly instincts told her things were not right with her baby girl.

During this time, my husband continued his store front face that displayed all was normal and okay. He went to church shortly after my mother arrived like the godly man who had everything handled. I was admitted back into the hospital that day from the emergency room. The doctors discovered I had an infection that consisted of multiple other infections the size of a baby.

I have always been and remain a hard person to locate a vein to stick and draw blood or start an IV. As if I was not tortured enough, they had to use a sonogram to find a vein deep in my arm to start an IV. Day-after-day, drawing blood, injecting medicine, getting CT scans, and having MRIs were full of pain and misery. The IVs would fail. Veins couldn't be found. Blood wouldn't come out. Veins would collapse, etc. Then, someone had the bright idea to call Rapid Response after the IV failed at the start of an MRI. The procedure to insert and thread a pic line up through my arm and near my heart was torture. But it was well worth the pain. The remainder of that week that I was in the hospital that pic line was used to draw blood, administer various antibiotics and medicine, inject dye for tests, and to dispense radiation.

Before I was discharged, I was informed that not only did I still have an infection that they were fighting; I had a mass on my kidney and a lesion on my liver. Something had to be done. But nothing would be done before the infection was gone. I was discharged under the care of Home Health. The God sent pic line was left in my arm because I had to have IV medicines inserted through it every eight hours around the clock when I was discharged to go home. And, I had a drain bag that the radiologist attached to my body to drain the infection constantly.

Guess what! My mom was the one who stayed at the hospital with me. She took me to and from the hospital. Yes, there were quite a bit of times she overstepped her boundaries or made comments unfit for my state of mind. Yet, she did the best she knew how in the hospital and to get me home while my spouse missed not one day at work.

My husband said it was the patients he couldn't leave even when decisions and procedures were necessary for me to be priority. I didn't know a twenty-two-year younger employee and the wife of a friend were the temptations that limited his visits and overnight stays.

Hearing me complain about my mom, my spouse accepted the opportunity not to be discovered by my mother. He had her to come by our family business to send her home with a monetary thank you for her services. I didn't want her negativity, but I didn't see the opportunity that, that gave my husband to isolate me. He was great about having church folks come and stay with me during the day and to drive me to appointments. Church family, friends, and neighbors provided us meals daily.

All of this worked perfectly for the image he portrayed that he was just hard at work to provide for his family. And, when he came home after work, they thought he was there to stay. On some Monday nights he'd leave me to go to his hometown church an hour and a half away. He'd go early and stay late, just like he had before I became sick. Other nights, he would claim to have a dental or vendor related meeting or something. Yet, on

> All of this worked perfectly for the image he portrayed that he was just hard at work to provide for his family.

Wednesday nights for our local church's Bible Study, he was excused not to attend under the auspices he was home taking care of me, his wife who still had a pic line inserted and getting around the clock doses of medicine through an IV. This was the case for many weeks.

Tuesday, October 17, 2017, in route for me to be admitted to the hospital to have surgery to remove the mass on my right kidney, the newest, young office mistress called. Unbeknownst to her, her Jezebel charming voice was projected through the Bluetooth in our Mercedes. Instead of greeting her male boss by utilizing the respect of his title, Dr. Cobbins, she said charmingly seductive, "Hhheeyyy." To give her a cue that he wasn't alone, he responded, "This is Dr. Cobbins. "Not catching or caring about his cue, she greeted him charmingly seductively again. He replied "Yeah, this is Dr. Cobbins. What's up?"

Though I was nervous about the impending surgery and that the removal of my whole right kidney could result, I thought she must be another trick to call her boss with that tone. I wondered if she called her boss at Walmart with that same tone. I felt so disrespected. I wondered besides conversations what else had been going on in my nearly eight-week absence from the office as of that date. I let it go because I didn't want my last words if I died to be anger about yet another mistress employee. Remember, I was his wife whose arm was still attached to an IV in route for major surgery.

We had a long wait before my kidney surgery started. We were given a 9:00 a.m. time but the doctor had not scheduled it until 12:45 p.m. My husband was frequently silent and mainly talked to our older gentleman friend. In addition to my parents, there were multiple people who came in and out to support me as we waited.

After I was prepped for surgery, my spouse saw a known black anesthesiologist was going to be a part of the surgery team taking care of me. My husband said that seeing that guy gave him peace. His countenance changed to be less reflective of being mad about getting caught about another mistress employee. It was like he instantly portrayed a good guy in front of a peer with whom he had worked to perform dental surgeries.

After I was in a room the night of my kidney surgery, I asked if the mass had been removed and whether I kept my kidney. My spouse said they had to remove part of the kidney to get all of the mass. I asked if that that meant I didn't have a right kidney. He said partially. That was sad and positive news too. The thing about this surgery is that my husband stayed overnight at the hospital with me in lieu of leaving. Trust that this was not the case for the rest of my week's hospital stay. Work or someone from work was calling which made him mainly absent. Yet, he was notorious to change his tone or countenance depending upon the setting or the person present.

Discovery of Yet Another Extra Marital Affair with an Employee in Our Family Business

There were more rough patches involving conversations about the finality of children during my recovery from three surgeries, radiologist procedures, and five hospital stays from the end of August to November. His issue became disgust as if I was worthless, because not only could I no longer have children, I refused to have conversations about adopting any. I was yet recovering myself, had a great provider but an absentee husband. By some miracle, with a pic line attached to me, I did whatever bookkeeping our CPA did not do while providing our business temporary assistance. I refused to put more on myself as a mother to more than my blood child and realized there was nothing my husband was going to do to increase his presence. And, if he felt like the business, profession, and church obligations required twelve hour shifts and weekend getaways of hunting and fishing for so called stress relief without our full family of three, how much more absences and pressure on me would it be if I agreed to increase our family size by adopting? And, it remained in my mind; I was married to a cheating man with whom the doctors still had not released me to have sex since August. That is before the first surgery. At this time, I was like the woman with the issue of blood. I was still having vaginal bleeding from the partial hysterectomy. And, I was not yet released to engage in sexual intercourse following my kidney surgery. Later, a second lesion on my liver was discovered.

The first time I was released to travel after my kidney surgery was for the Christmas trip with my husband's side of the family. We went to Destin, Florida for the annual vacation that I initiated way back in 2007. Though the doctor provided me restrictions, I was happy just to go.

Prior to leaving, my husband got us new

phones and service with C-Spire. The service was some kind of terrible in Destin. And, though he always said that was his time to relax and do nothing but enjoy being in the same house with his parents, siblings, and their off springs, he was noticeably distant and responded to me rudely even in the presence of his family.

I had coordinated him a camouflaged appreciation for the family to celebrate the fact that annually he's carried the responsibility for lodging. This included the monetary cost until others, who would, reimbursed him. His mood fluctuated between happy and displeasure, at the time, for no apparent reason. It didn't stop me from posting us to social media in our attire with his side of our family.

During that trip we learned that his relative had recently married a much younger lady. My father-in-law made the statement that the relative messed up with that because that age difference would be something to handle. He didn't know that my husband was juggling the same problem with his twenty-two-year younger mistress employee. She was the employee who I mentioned earlier had called him in route to my kidney surgery.

The Storm Continues...

Well, our bad C-Spire service didn't stop my husband from using his various personal and business phones to keep in touch with that employee who he nicknamed "Sunshine." He was smart enough to disable the notifications from her, but that was about it. He was so smitten with her that he used a fake concern for the mistress employee's dog "Kenny Baby" as a reason to contact her. (This was a house dog for her. Since then, the lover boss demoted it to an outside dog at his nicer place.) And, to keep up with her goings on during our trip, he inquired about how what he called a Christmas party at her mom's had gone. He used all kinds of deceptive interest to keep their communication going since texting he missed her was insufficient.

The bombshell and flirtatious conversations that were in the eye of the Tornado/storm included the text communication between my husband and his mistress employee where he asked her to file insurance to get him approved for Lipo suction. He told her he hoped she would be more attracted to him if his stomach was no longer big. Consistent with a Jezebel spirit, she opted to continue the conversation with a known married man old enough to be her daddy and gave him advice on a cheaper way to lose the weight. But, she was intentional to let him know she knew he had the money and could pay.

My husband tried deleting text from our 2017 Christmas trip and earlier with that particular mistress. Pictures he had taken of the mistress employee in compromising positions at the locations where she assists him to conduct dental procedures and pictures side-by-side after our business' Christmas party right before our family Christmas trip were enough to show me, I was no longer valued as the prize he asked to marry.

I saw on our three-member family trip to New Orleans, after the 2017 Christmas trip with my husband's side of the family, that the mistress employee had been using both my husband's personal and business cell phones to take and store selfies. What kind of woman does that knowing the man she is after is married and whose wife worked in the same business until prolonged sickness

> What kind of woman does that knowing that the man she is after is married and whose wife worked in the same business until prolonged sickness after recent surgeries?

after recent surgeries?

(Sidebar: Know that telephone and text records are discoverable. You can do research now using your access to online accounts. Plus, there are means by which you can recover what has been deleted. The mobile carrier will not have a record of photos and videos and social media correspondences (like Messenger, etc.) But, if you have a careless cheater who engages with someone who has a jezebel spirit, trust that there are additional phones, Inbox correspondences, photos, and videos that will make you sick to your stomach. Be wise. As much as you may want to fuss and tell what you discovered, do not! I repeat. DO NOT!!! This does not exclude those you think you can trust. It's amazing who will turn on you and who shows support. And, once things start unfolding, you may be surprised with whom (right under your nose) your spouse is cheating.)

I didn't have a suspicion of the friend's wife. Yet, my heart confirmed this was yet another mistress employee right under my nose. Like the friend's wife, the employee pretended to be respectful towards me. I couldn't decide which mistress employee was worse. Like the previous, I felt she should be fired. Knowing he would disagree, I took matters into my own hands and carried it out. But he reversed it, and she didn't hesitate to return to the employment of her lover boss.

I prayed that she reaped what she had been sowing. And, I couldn't understand how once again the preacher, anointed speaker, Bible scholar for which I was married could continue to fall so easily to the devil's tactics. I started rationalizing and remembered what he shared in church once while preaching. He talked about being a country boy whose heart was broken by a high school sweetheart. He claimed he went to a game and saw his high school girlfriend with another man. I had never heard this before he told the whole congregation. Knowing the latest mistress employee was not his first episode, I wondered if every time he cheated, he was internally getting back at his high school sweetheart. Consistent with others in our families, my husband chose to engage in the same adulterous activities. For far too long I had forgotten my value is far above rubies. I ignored the Biblical reasons I had to proceed with a divorce filing.

> For far too long I had forgotten my value is far above rubies.

The Storm Continues...

January 2018, I visited a lawyer. The lawyer heard my story and gave me things to expect based on her divorce experience and connected me with a private investigator who was familiar with my husband's side of the family. I paid the retainer to start the divorce process.

It's not you. Yes, you and I are imperfect people wanting perfect mates. Never think for some reason your inability to have children or unwillingness to adopt children encourages a spouse to cheat and continue it with any trick, thot, jezebel, innocent person, etc.

If you are like I was and are in a relationship with a known liar, you are enabling a cheater. We are flawed and have work to do. Yet, we are more valuable than being lied to and cheated on by those we married or committed to in advance of marriage.

> We are flawed and have work to do.

Plus, I tend to disagree with the saying, Keep your friends close and your enemies closer. Those who allowed my spouse to use their vehicle to visit mistresses and the now known wife who engaged in a sexual relationship with him deserve no seat at my table or future business.

NOTES

What Have or Are You Gleaning from Your Current or Previous Relationship "In The Storm?"_____

_____

_____

_____

_____

_____

_____

_____

_____

_____

_____

_____

_____

The Storm Continues...

Coming Out of The Storm

When the storm is long gone from the area, its affect and signs linger forever.

The Aftermath

After the storm hits, folks outside of an area can be misled if they don't or can't take the time to visit the affected area. Listening to or watching the news reports summarizing the damage and seeing the limited pictures and stories are insufficient for a realistic view. Damage reaches beyond what the eyes may see. Such lackadaisical concern is why many rarely realize a tornado has caused lifelong destruction.

> Damage reaches beyond what the eyes may see.

This is what happened after the tornado hit and the impending divorce began. Most people with whom we had personal and overlapping relationships now considered one or both of us a casualty of the storm. Those who didn't have this view have reflected action or inaction as to which one of us they will support in the rebuilding. Let's take a closer look at a few.

The Façade to the Church

Sunday-after-Sunday initially, we would go to church as if nothing happened. Church members were used to us riding to church together and separately on a periodic basis. Please remember I was married to a good window dresser. When we didn't ride together, they would assume he had to go speak at another church, had a meeting, or something else valid. They didn't know he was making pit stops meeting up with a mistress employee and others. When I didn't have my own Sunday School class to conduct, I would try to be late to Sunday School because I didn't want to sit in the class of my Sunday School teacher, who was also my adulterous husband.

It would literally make me sick in my head and stomach hearing him teach Sunday School knowing what he was teaching was far from him. I think the part of his teaching that kept him comfortable to remain in his positions of teacher and Elder was that there is no condemnation in those who love God, and that Jesus paid the price for our sins (past, present, and future.)

The Façade to the Family

Approximately February of 2018, my nephew contacted me in advance of contacting my husband, the preacher. My nephew sought and received my husband's agreement to counsel and marry his now lovely wife in September of that year. Initially, my husband told him he may not be able to do it because of a conflict. I back peddled on encouraging him to do it thinking that he'd be convicted and repent for his multiple ongoing adulterous acts. And so, he agreed.

Four months later and seeing my spouse was being enabled to continue the inappropriate relationship with the employee and not making sizable efforts to restore our marriage, I confided in a family member. The feedback was hard. I was told because females in my family made me a strong-willed woman, I was not able to see the small efforts that my husband was making. This person believed the spirit showed that my husband had grown weary trying. Nothing in me could accept that any issue with me warranted standing by and seeing an inappropriate relationship with a mistress

> The feedback was hard.

employee or other mistresses maintained.

After I missed my husband's family reunion, I had the opportunity to tell my mother-in-love we were divorcing when she called to check on not having heard from me. She had absolutely no clue. He had not told her. Though I suspected the siblings knew because of pictures and communications I witnessed, my mother-in-love said they told her that she wasn't wearing her hearing aid because she couldn't have heard me correctly. When one of them questioned my husband about their mother's news, he had the nerve to text me as if chastising me in his route home from "a meeting." Included in the text, he said he didn't want things to be hard on me when we both had a need to show up at either side's future events. I guess he thought I was going to let him manipulate and control me during and after the divorce as he had become accustomed to doing in our marriage. Or, he knew what I am now experiencing. That is, that his side of the family would ostracize me even though I have not done a thing. He also knew they would stand by him based on examples he followed obviously.

When his mom called back, she said to call her anytime that I had not done a thing to her. She told me don't let my husband go for some woman just because of hearsay. When I gave her details and she shared her story, she concluded their pastor didn't know and needed to counsel her baby boy instead of her baby counseling other folks. Since then, I received one call from my former mother-in-love and that was to check on our son who had gotten hurt while at her house. The same mistress employee that she asked me not to leave her son for has been welcomed in her presence, home, and on the Destin family trip I initiated.

The night before my August 2018 after work and unexpected admission to the hospital, I felt the need to communicate with my parents that I filed for a divorce. My nephew's wedding was fast approaching and taking place on the weekend following Labor Day. And, I wanted to know based on my husband's actions and potential to not show up for the wedding if they thought I should tell my nephew so there would be a backup plan. I thought it was bad enough my nephew and his fiancé had been coming into our house for counseling and had no clue we had started the process to divorce. (This was because I was intentional to have things to do away from the house when I knew their counseling times and dates. Unlike the previous couple my husband married, I didn't participate in my nephew and his wife's marital counseling.) My parents and I agreed, if my husband had a change of mind about officiating the wedding, that it would be my husband's responsibility to tell it.

After being in the emergency room by myself so late after work, my son who knew all of our divorce business called and became worried that I was at the hospital. He contacted my mother and she checked on me. I thought I was going to receive some medicine and be released knowing I had just one month prior started a new job.

The Lord allowed my husband's cousin and a neighbor to join me at the hospital. The cousin followed my neighbor to my home (the second mansion for which we were living) as the neighbor drove my vehicle. When the cousin got items for me to have at the hospital from my husband, he questioned who was with me and asked if my mom knew. He told her that no matter what we were going through he still loved me and could stay at the hospital with me. (Tee hee. What do you think? Was that window dressing or did that have a different motive? He is the same man who had just spent the day with his mistress employee and text me (the wife with whom he was living and in the process of a divorce.) In his text, he told me I didn't need to cook for him that evening because he was not going to be home after work and would be eating elsewhere. After two surgeries and radiologist procedures during that admission, he text me over in the night one of my sickest overnight hospital stays to inquire if I told my nephew about the divorce process because he didn't want to mess up their wedding day. I hadn't. But, as usual, he was only concerned about how he looked. (That trait is notorious for those who are queens and kings of window dressing.) Following discharge and readmission, he put on such a good show for my parents who came to visit me at the hospital. That led them to question me as to whether we were really getting a divorce. Instead of my parents staying at the hospital with me during what was the Labor Day and family reunion weekend, my spouse volunteered and stayed multiple nights with me. He was there to drive me when I was discharged on Labor Day. Immediately following my nephew's wedding, the next Saturday, my spouse left for a two-night

> But, as usual, he was only concerned about how he looked.

fishing trip out-of-state. He gave no thought to childcare for our son being left with me, the helpless mom.

After the divorce process was known, my spouse's side of the family made it blatantly clear that they were on his side even if he was the one who had done the wrong. They have accepted the lies he told them that my mother and brother put him out of the house and that I had stolen his money. My then spouse never showed his family his text to me where he agreed to pick up his items from the side porch under protected covering. Just because my mother and brother were present when he arrived that October day, he used his window dressing trait as an opportunity to paint a picture of them falsely. In fact, my brother offered and my then spouse accepted my brother's help with loading his things (all packed by non-family.) (I was still recovering from a surgery and a readmission.)

The Storm Continues...

On my side, I, to this day, have family who verbally support me and are quite supportive of my ex and make nice comments publicly about his additional off springs. Sometimes that has felt insulting and showed me I still have some growing. Otherwise, our families and friends' actions in support of my ex would have zero effect on me.

> Sometimes that has felt insulting and showed me I still have some growing.

What tickled me is when my ex called and wished my grandmother a Happy Mother's Day during our divorce process. This is the same person he didn't like to be around. She made it known each time she saw him he had gained weight. And, he always bit his tongue with her like he does with others to keep from admitting that he only likes the taste of his immediate family's fried corn.

The Half-Hearted Attempt to Salvage the Marriage

After my January 2018 visit to an attorney and talks with once trusted friends, my husband agreed for us to participate in marriage sessions with them. Though he agreed to that, never would he commit to releasing his mistress employee.

Over a month, he said it was best that I work from home so she could be comfortable and not quit. As a concession, one day he told me to come to the office so he could apologize to each of us in front of the other. I guess they both thought I was crazy to not think she was not in on his plot to give him more time and ensure things didn't get messier. In front of her, my husband told me, "I'm sorry for the embarrassment this has caused you." In front of me, he told the mistress employee, "I'm sorry for my advances and thank you for not accepting them." After I persisted, he called the mistress employee back to his office and said she would no longer be allowed to play with his phones. She smiled and said ok. Then, she looked at me and said, "That's my bad about the phones."

I am sure I was the laughingstock of the office. Go back and read the apology I said my husband, who was supposed to be attempting to save our marriage, gave me. This was the same preacher who was concerned enough that he looked like the Pillsbury Dough man to text his mistress employee about lipo over the Christmas break. That is the same man who at our company Christmas party sat and took pictures side-by-side the mistress employee at the restaurant. And, he is the same

The Storm Continues...

man who followed the mistress employee and the others out of the restaurant as he told me to stay put for him to pull the car up closer for me. He took that opportunity to go outside the restaurant to stop the mistress employee to take more pictures without ever mentioning what he had done before I saw the pictures. Be reminded, they had taken ample pictures in the restaurant in my presence.

During the workday prior to the arrival at the restaurant, the mistress employee had taken selfie pictures using her lover boss' phone some of which she included her co-workers while I, the wife was home and not released to work. So, the employees all knew about the affair. And, one has been employed during the employment of other mistress employees. A married co-worker stayed all night with the mistress employee after our business' Christmas party. She has commented on one of the mistress employee's social media post that the mistress employee is wifely material. (Why would she make such comment if the mistress employee didn't have an M.O. for being a side chick to my married man or another in a committed relationship? Likewise, why would the mistress employee caption a different post of herself with, "She doesn't compete. No one compares." Such deliberate message is telling of someone seeking or waiting to be another's replacement.)

My husband wanted me to believe none of the other employees knew about their secret. He said those who had children out of wedlock, a relationship with a married man, or a work friendship with his mistress employee didn't know what he and the mistress employee had going on. He maintained it was not known by any employee even when he, the mistress employee, and another employee went to Hoover, Alabama for a dental conference while I was sick following my kidney surgery. The Lord gave him a way of escape that he didn't take in route to that conference. See our son and the church lady staying with us contacted him about our refrigerator was leaking uncontrollably. Instead of turning around and taking care of his family himself, he sent a younger and older friend to work on the refrigerator and get up the water. It was no way he was going to miss an opportunity for two nights and three days away with the 22-year younger mistress employee.

After discovering the inappropriate relationship, I did a drop in to our office. I saw the mistress employee putting on my husband's gloves for him in the operatory with a relative who was being seen as a patient. I had him to put an end to that. Later, you'll read how he tested this disrespectfully.

On Valentine's Day, my husband didn't come home nor invite me for lunch. Therefore, I had no choice but to believe he had a Valentine's lunch with his mistress employee. I became fed up and made a big deal about him obviously showing the mistress employee he chose her over me. I fussed going inside the church to make it obvious to the Assistant Pastor, whom I had already confided in, about my husband's most recent adulterous activities. It only resulted in a late Valentine's night post by my husband with pictures of me and words to window dress his acknowledgment of me being his Valentine.

To test my husband's commitment to try and save our marriage, I asked him to take off from our business and take a week's trip to Las Vegas. He agreed. Even on that trip, his communication with the mistress employee continued. And, he still refused to commit to fire her.

When we returned from the trip, the mistress employee told her lover boss that she had a wreck in her Mercedes. (Do you really believe her dental assistant job at our business and her job at Walmart was sufficient to pay for a Mercedes and to live solo in a gated apartment complex? A lot of men who cheat do it successfully when they have money. It's the bait they use to buy and sustain their women. Plus, some women look for a sugar daddy.) My husband asked me if I wanted to return her call or be on the call with him when he responded to her request for time off. I knew they had and would be in private communication. Therefore, I gave him the opportunity to make the right decision for me, the HR Manager of our business, to handle what didn't fall under the purview of the practicing dentist. Welp, he chose wrong. He chose to communicate and check in with his mistress employee privately.

Annually at Spring break, we use to take off all or part of the week to take our son somewhere out-of-state. During this period when he had committed to working on saving the marriage, my husband said he had to work and earn money since he had missed a week in February to go to Vegas.

The Storm Continues...

Money was no issue and he encouraged me to use as much as I wanted to, to take our son on a Spring Break trip anyway. I decided to go by our office before leaving for the trip. You guessed it. I got to witness the ex and his mistress employee enjoying one another's company at work together.

After the April Canton Flea Market, my husband didn't want me in the office after his mistress employee and the co-workers, who were definitely in on their affair, returned from lunch. When I left, I immediately returned. Appearing like his arm was around me, he used it to push on me down the hall and out of the office. He did this instead of hugging me and speaking sweet nothings to me for the mistress employee and the other employees could hear and see as I requested so stupidly.

Prior to that incident, I had gone to our office and saw written on the board in the office that the mistress employee had made her own, "The Most Beautiful Dental Assistant." I asked her about it, and she claimed a co-worker had written it. I told her it needs to be erased and had no place in this office with a man she wants who's married. She said she didn't want anybody. I said

> She said she didn't want anybody.

you are lying, or you wouldn't still be here knowing he's married and the problems you're causing. I told her if she wanted to have the conversation in front of the boss we could because what I am saying stands. She said she didn't. No soon as she erased the board and I was out of her sight, she went and reported me, the wife, and HR Manager, to our boss, her twenty-two-year older lover. As the two were coming out of his office, I saw the distress on both of their faces. I asked if she wanted an order. Before, I could get "from McAlister's" out she said she didn't. I asked him if he had a problem. He didn't want to talk about it. Yet, he was quick to report to friends the person he suspected had called me and told me what was on the board leading to my appearance at the office. And, he told them I said something to the mistress employee. He never said that the best way to end this issue with the mistress employee is to end her employment relationship. Instead of showing me there was no longer anything going on, when I returned with the food, the mistress employee came in the ortho room to assist my husband. He held his hands out for her to put his gloves on. When he came out of the room, I told him he was testing me with that act, and he should be happy that the mistress employee didn't fall for it. I said if she is putting on her gloves and staying sterile, you can put yours on and stay sterile. It's bad enough y'all sitting here catching feels by bumping knees behind the patients' backs. Fortunately, for us, the mistress employee didn't take his bait to put his gloves on. She handed him the gloves to do himself.

Then, there was our 23rd wedding anniversary cruise in May that my husband got his dental society executive assistant to book for us. We couldn't be on the seven-day cruise without the mistress employee and him texting. I bumped into this information when he gave me his phone for another purpose. He pretended like they only communicated about her asking to leave work early.

(Hint: Ladies and gentlemen, if there is an extra-marital working relationship concern and your mate wants to rebuild your trust, there will be no secrets that you bump into. All cards will be laid on the table. The mate who betrayed the marital trust will go overboard to reassure and regain trust from

> The mate who betrayed the marital trust will go overboard to reassure and regain trust from the other mate.

the other mate.)

But such half-hearted attempts again showed me the messed-up dude I was waiting and hoping would come to his senses and the value I lost for myself. It's him to blame, period. She couldn't do any more than he allowed. Trust me she is completely, absolutely, 200% guilty. Yet, her twenty-two-year older, lover, boss had far more time and experience to exceed any of her tricks, conveyed as her innocence. Staying focused, it was with him whom I was married and accepted the halfhearted attempts and serial cheating.

Come on Sisters! Ask yourself these questions: What is it? Do I think I am not worthy of being treated like Christ commanded the husband to love his wife? Is this the normal that is healthy for me? Is this the value I have for myself? Am I scared I may end up with someone worse or no one at all?

Quest for a New Employer

At this time and to their satisfaction, I had no desire to return to our dental practice during the same hours the mistress employee and my husband were there. And, he absolutely refused to fire her. Remember, I told

The Storm Continues...

you he apologized to the two of us. Nothing in that apology was restoration for me into my rightful place in our business or to be committed to only me, the woman with whom he was married.

He told me that if I got an additional job, I could use that money for myself as long as I did the work I had to do for the family business. Initially, he said that I should contribute my pay from a new employer to our family funds so that he could get his vision started to buy an additional practice. He said if something happened affecting our business it would be best that all of our income was not dependent upon that source, that is, the family dental practice. I was like, are you crazy?! Do you really want me to get another job and put the money into our joint funds to help fund a new location for our family business for which I can't be present?!

Realizing he was making plans that gave him more time away with his mistress employee and having seen her playing with the pediatric patients; hearing her discuss care for her relative's children; and recalling his desire for and our conversations about children, I knew she had cast her net to catch him at her childbearing age. And, I said but if he gets with her, they are going to be in the same situation he acted like he was trying to prevent. Remember, he said he didn't want all of our funds to come from one pot if something happened. At this time, the mistress employee no longer worked at Walmart and was getting all of her funds and benefits from her dentist, daddy-aged boss, and lover.

> Remember, he said he didn't want all of our funds to come from one pot if something happened.

This was writing I saw on the wall. I applied, interviewed, and made contacts with those in my professional networks. Then thankfully, The Lord allowed me to receive an offer for a job while we were on my husband's birthday trip in Seattle, WA. This was one of those on-time prayer answers. Because a couple of days prior to the trip, my husband and I agreed things were not working and to move forward with the divorce.

Mister Window Dresser went on that trip and played his part like usual. Around his family, who were on the trip, he would reference me as "my wife;" placed his arms around my waist, slept in the same bed with me vs our son; and pulled out his wallet to pay for everything as usual like food, all of our shopping, and admission into to all kinds of touristy places.

Ladies, this is a true master manipulator at its finest. He knew this would send mixed signals to me and make me not willing to fight for what I deserved during the divorce process. Well, before we could get off the airplane good back in Jackson, Mississippi the Monday morning after his birthday, he powered on his phones. As we were walking through the terminal, the mistress employee called him to see what time he would be at the office. That was my sign from God to stay the course and don't get blindsided by the deception tactic my manipulative husband had just used that weekend.

> That was my sign from God to stay the course and don't get blindsided by the deception tactic my manipulative husband had just used that weekend.

Is that similar to your situation? Why is it we cannot be our sister's keeper? We know a man is in a marriage or a relationship. We know he has a reputation for cheating. Yet, ladies participate or wait willingly for their turn in line. Or, we stay with the man just to say we still have that particular man or any man at all. We take bad risks knowing we are not the

> We prefer gifts and finer living over sound judgment.

The Divorce Filing had been on my new job for one month. I was still being paid to conduct the work for the family business. Yet, I had suggested that our CPA's office should conduct the accounting work because it was too hard for me to see documents and produce pay for the mistress employee. My husband was agreeable to this idea. And, he promised to continue my same pay from the family business to stay off site so the mistress employee would remain, feel comfortable, and not quit.

Having separate pay to fall on in case my husband decided to pull the plug from my pay, I was in a better position to seek an attorney. Then I pondered, why use my separate earnings? I know my husband has money to afford women, our second mansion, businesses, luxury vehicles, destination vacations, etc. For a time, I

> For a time, I chanced following an attorney's advice to let my husband pay the price to get the key to the life he wanted.

chanced following an attorney's advice to let my husband pay the price to get the key to the life he wanted.

Unbeknownst to me, he had been in contact with a lawyer. This lawyer was referred to him by his fraternity brother, who is a lawyer.

The lawyer/fraternity brother happens to be the brother-in-law to one of the females with whom my husband cheated on me while we were in college. Although the lawyer friend and his wife have been in our Mississippi homes and are on pictures celebrating with us during our various events, he became the lawyer for my husband's mistress employee in my case against her.

It was like déjà vu. When the fraternity brother, my husband (then boyfriend,) and I, were in undergraduate school and the two of them lived in a rental house together, this fraternity brother brought the sister of his girlfriend (now wife) to my boyfriend's family reunion. I had come to the reunion with my boyfriend.

At the end of the reunion weekend, my boyfriend and I returned to our college/my hometown. While at my boyfriend and his fraternity brother's rental house, I asked the fraternity brother why he brought his girlfriend's sister to the family reunion knowing that wasn't right.

25 years later, I saw the same fraternity brother, turned lawyer; serve as the attorney for my spouse's mistress employee in our case. I had the same question, i.e. Why would you do that knowing the situation? Yet, I never asked. His support and involvement years later are eye opening and a real-life example of a "my brother's keeper" that others should not imitate.

One Sunday, after seeing account funds written in the mistress employee's handwriting, I let my husband have it when I saw him outside the church. He told me we would talk at home.

It took night to come for him to collect the thoughts and to initiate the conversation. He kept denying there was not a relationship between the two. He had forgotten he had let out in a conversation before that it was just the sex. Nor did he know I had the proof that I had. So instead of me being accepting of our marriage just being over, I wanted him to explain and choose me. I got his phone and saw he had been snooping the mistress employee and others' Facebook pages. He had the address and had paid a fee to the lawyer recommended by his fraternity brother, the lawyer.

When he tried to take the phone from me, I went Live so the young Jezebel, mistress employee and the other woman could see their sex man was home with his wife. He tried too rough to take his phone from me.

When I put the phone down, I pretended like I was calling the police. Unfortunately, our son saw the Live and came to our room and saw how his dad was holding me. I left out of the room but told our son I would make a pretend call to the police to get his dad's attention. This was a bad decision on my part. Our son had already endured seeing evidence and being present for a lot of the support for the grounds of our divorce. Added to that, our son witnessed time-after-time his dad sleeping in one room, then sleeping in the room with me, saying we were going to stay a family, changing to say things are not working, the interactions between his dad and the mistress employee on-the-job.

When I pretended like I was talking to the police, I did it such that my husband could hear me. He got dressed and packed a bag. He told our son in response that he was probably going to be asked to leave when the police arrived. I admitted I was pretending and that I hadn't called the police. I said I made a mistake because all I ever wanted was for you to choose me. He looked in disbelief.

The next morning, I went in the room where my husband was and asked if he was sure he didn't want to try and work things out. He hesitated a moment and then said no. Knowing he had paid and talked to a reputable attorney, I decided I had best to choose one of the attorneys I had recently interviewed and not go back to the attorney to whom I paid a retainer in January.

Before I arrived to work, I started getting crazy text from my husband containing pictures of a scratched-up arm and saying I never loved him and only was after his money. I told him he had to be desperate to do that to himself and to try to blame his rough handling me as if I had done something to him. I knew the clock was ticking and his strategy was unfolding.

The Storm Continues...

I called my chosen attorney and told him what happened and gave him the name of my husband's anticipated attorney. He knew him and told me what I needed to do to start the divorce filing. The big problem was that he saw money because he knew my husband's profession. The attorney told me based on my husband's status and the time it may take to get the divorce finalized that I needed to withdraw the funds to cover my anticipated attorney fees (at a minimum.) From his experience, spouses cut off one another's access to accounts during a divorce process. I was scared and didn't want to do that. I talked with those I thought I could trust and who had wisdom and even the person I felt was siding with my husband. They all told me, since the divorce was inevitable, to do it. It was a marital asset, and my name was on the account. I prayed and withdrew the money and simultaneously filed for divorce from my husband and alienation of affection against the

> The attorney told me based on my husband's status and the time it may take to get the divorce finalized that I needed to withdraw the funds to cover my anticipated attorney fees (at a minimum.)

mistress employee. I am choosing to allow the sexual relationship to unfold with the others, especially the married woman. Intuition, carelessness, and time will reveal all in the closet activities. I won't have any parts in it. Children, others, and ultimately the body of Christ will be impacted. I have seen for myself and will continue to believe the scripture that says for nothing is covered that will not be revealed.

If this is similar to a situation you are going through, know that you are wearing an invisible band aid on an intangible wound. You are going to have to hurt before you heal. The healing WILL BE painful. To start the process, you have to yank off that band aid. Otherwise, you are letting the infection grow bigger. Sometimes, you feel like you are helping a situation by covering it to soothe you. In a case as bad as this one, you have to uncover it so you can get oxygen to breathe and heal. Don't die in this. Greater is coming.

> The healing WILL BE painful. To start the process, you have to yank off that band aid.

Assessing the Damage

How do you know if you have sustained damage from a storm? The first means generally involves a self-assessment of the area. Some things can't be reviewed independently. An insurance adjuster has to survey the area. Otherwise, soon you'll notice leaks or worse a roof may cave in. In these sections, I'll discuss the results of personal and other assessments from this storm's damage. You'll want to continue reading. Soon you'll learn that damage is not confined to one area.

> Soon you'll learn that damage is not confined to one area.

Divorce Cares Support Group

Immediately, I knew I needed some repairs. The barrage and combination of emotions had me angry, sad, depressed, anxious, abandoned, isolated, etc. And, because these feelings showed up out-of-nowhere or could be triggered by simple things like grocery shopping, vacations, and tv shows, I felt no one who were once thought of as couple friends understood my experience; could be trusted; initiated time with me; or showed me care and concern. I needed to be heard and to share information in a safe space. For me, that looked like a place where I did not feel judged or alone.

After some research, it was like The Lord revealed various churches in the area that hosted a Divorce Cares Support Group. This male and female group consisted of those who were anticipating filing for divorce; had filed but not completed the divorce process; and others who had been divorced for some time but who had not completed the work required in the initial years after the divorce to heal and recover.

I became sick a second time mid-way the 13-week session and missed several weeks of in-person lessons. I was still able to graduate and feel I got the gist of the sessions and am fortunate it came with a workbook. Like others who were in my group, I feel comfortable to repeat the sessions in the future if or when needed.

Health Issues Resurface

As I alluded to in previous sections, I have had bouts of health issues. The tornado that hit with my first serious health issue was an EF5. Its aftermath produced subsequent hits in the form of hospitalizations and sickness that year and the year afterwards.

The Storm Continues...

Doctors and lay people say that stress is a trigger for major illnesses. Please take it from me. Divorce is a severe stress inducer.

> Doctors and lay people say that stress is a trigger for major illnesses.

I have always been one who lost weight when I was stressed and worried. I had not recovered the weight I lost from the previous year during my sickness before confirming my husband's inappropriate relationship with the mistress employee. After the divorce process began, I lost more weight that I didn't have to lose. And, my husband lost the weight he had tried to lose previously but struggled to do for the mistress employee.

Effect on the Child

My, my, my, my, my! Bless the little children. Please know that a child loves both parents. They are not dumb. They will often think the divorce was because of something they did or should have done. Or, they are pulled between both parents for loyalty when all the child wants to do is save the family.

> Please know that a child loves both parents.

Prior to the knowledge of the most recent mistress employee, our son saw her as his friend and the closest in age at our family business. Once the information was known, our son felt betrayed. He struggled between disliking the person he saw as his peer to wanting her as a friend but not family. Through her and his dad's adulterous acts, my son now has siblings. He loves them dearly. Yet, he fluctuates with how he feels about the now girlfriend employee because of the many lies he was told by his daddy denying their relationship adamantly to her being thrust in his face and forced to accept as an innocent person to his two-parent family household's demise.

The effect on our child has reared its head in rebellion, disrespect, incomplete assignments, and similar challenges exacerbated in teenagers and the current ways of the world. Amidst all of these, our son is still told right from wrong. This has been a hard pill for him to swallow. The daily reminders of the lies our son's dad told him stare in his face. This is because our son's dad resorted to shacking up in our second mansion with the same girlfriend employee and their babies conceived before the divorce was final. And, our son lives with his dad.

The Storm Continues...

On the other hand, there are the many wonderful effects on the child. They include growth, maturity, love, care, concern, and hard work. Our son has actually picked up an entrepreneurial trait and striving to become self-sufficient. Some say, had our son not been a victim of our divorce, we still would have observed him experiencing challenges and rewards of growing up.

The Family's Response

I touched on this in depth in other sections. It is worth repeating here. In a storm, the true sides of family will be revealed.

> In a storm, the true sides of family will be revealed.

In the case of my ex, his side supports him 98%. Their lack of reaching out to me appears as their signs of loyalty to him.

My former mother-in-love has embraced her youngest two grandchildren (currently) and their mother (her baby boy's girlfriend employee. Though both of the youngest two were conceived before our divorce was final, the last was given the last name Cobbins at birth.) All of that is what it is. I am only confused about why any of it prevents an arm's length relationship with me, the mother of the baby boy's first child and with whom there had not been relationship challenges. No acknowledgment of the sincere card I mailed to show care and concern during and to my former in-laws' COVID sickness reinforced my concern.

Of my ex's siblings, I have communicated with one. It was a brief and cordial conversation. I was told the phone called me accidentally. I do not believe in happenstance. I think it was meant to be. That sibling is the one who had stated in the hallway during the divorce trial that I had blocked all contact to me in response to my comment that they had not reached out to me. Social media was the only place I blocked them. This was to ensure my healing. The life any of them were living or displaying on social media needed no space in my eyes or mind. So, I believed the "accidental phone call" was God's way of allowing that sibling to see the means of contacting me was the same as it was before the divorce filing.

On the other hand, my side has been 70% supportive and loyal to me. My basis for this percentage was discussed in an earlier chapter. Just know I had a false expectation of at least 90% support and loyalty from my family.

Even if you are also blessed to have a 25 year and 10-month marriage and a decent relationship with your in-laws, do not be surprised if the ex's family stops dealing with you completely. This can prove to be the case even if you are not responsible for the marriage downfall. Likewise, do not expect your side of the family to have an allegiance with you solely. Nope, that is not 100% likely. And, honestly it shows immaturity for us to expect this. You or your ex didn't wrong each other's family members.

Like unrelated people, family members can be opportunist. Some will try to maintain connections with the one who has the most money, power, and status, right or wrong.

The Church's Response

This was the one place I was totally blown away. I had heard it happens. I pray this was my last time experiencing it.

Men in ministry can be known in the church for committing fornication and adultery. And, they may get to maintain their position and leadership over God's children.

> Men in ministry can be known in the church for committing fornication and adultery.

Some become like magnets who attract even more women. We everyday Christians are taught to be careful what we do because the very appearance of a thing could lead a person of the faith astray.

Since my ex is an ordained elder, we would utilize such <u>Bible</u> teaching when counseling others. In the marriage counseling that the ex and I conducted of couples before they wed, we made a primary request. We asked each couple to abstain from sex before marriage. In the case of the couple we counseled, who had the largest gap between ages, we also tried to forewarn and prepare them for the challenges to be expected by the more than a decade difference in their ages. I just didn't know, at that time, what we were teaching varied from my husband's beliefs, though there were previous episodes of his experiments.

The churches where my ex holds ministry roles knew and still know the lifestyle my ex leads. He spoke since I left the church where his membership resides. I understood that he conveyed that his act of adultery was a mistake and shared other lies when announcing the first child he conceived with his girlfriend employee before the dissolution of the marriage. The church since learned that it wasn't a mistake. It is a lifestyle he has chosen, without repentance, as proven by the conception of their second child before the divorce was final. Instead, he continues in ministry, preaching, and leading others astray while shacking up.

When I left the church, my ex attends and later found a church home to transfer my and our son's membership, I could not knowingly sit under my ex's ministry practices, continue his request to keep our life and impending divorce a secret, and live a lie before our church family. I was given my letter with no issue. I choose to believe if I was the one with the pocket of money, the church leaders would have initiated at least one approach to encourage or check on me and our son in an attempt for us to stay.

Though I served in roles at the church too, I caused the church no shame. However, I didn't garner much support for the divorce decision that I had made. Ladies with wisdom made comments like all men cheat in hopes that I would stay in a marriage consisting of adultery. That is a reason for divorce that God allows.

> Ladies with wisdom made comments like all men cheat in hopes that I would stay in a marriage consisting of adultery.

Some of their whispered and loud stories of enduring adulterous marriages led them to ignore I had tried far too long to stay in my marriage to an unfaithful man who they may view and respect highly.

The Staff in The Family Dental Practice's Response

The attorneys warned me that no matter how good of a business person I was nor if I was liked by the employees that our employees would maintain allegiance with the spouse who is the focus of the business. Though turnover has taken place there, most of the employees who were present during the start of the divorce remain employed. I have had no communications with the other employees who remain employed at the dental practice since I left. This is exclusive of a birthday text exchange.

The girlfriend employee has been elevated formally as Lead Dental Assistant and is openly known as the boss' younger woman and mother of his youngest children. Besides our correspondences via the legal system for the case, that I dropped, I and the girlfriend employee have no communication. She actually has been a blessing in disguise in so many ways that I originally could not see and she likely didn't intend. Other than the poor example to the Christian community and visual aid for my son, I care less that she is shacking up with my ex in our former marital domicile in the presence of their children.

It is my prayer that the spirit that is in operation against families at that practice will be one day cast off before others in and outside of the business are impacted. It's one thing to make a mistake. It's a difference when a preacher who is the leader of the business leads the way for inappropriate relationships and lifestyles inconsistent with what he reads and teaches from The Holy Bible. No one is exempt. The devil doesn't care who he attacks. He dug his heels deep at that dental practice. Loving everyone should continue but conforming should not.

———————
No one is exempt. The devil doesn't care who he attacks.
———————

Counseling

Counseling played a part in the storm and after the storm. This was key for me and my son.

There is a stigma in a lot of communities, social statuses, amongst genders, and across races applied to those who seek counseling. All I am going to say is kick other people's perception out of your mind. You need to do what you can do to navigate the pain and process to get through the storm.

> You need to do what you can do to navigate the pain and process to get through the storm.

There are counselors for almost everything. Some locations have counselors who charge based on a fee scale. Pray that God leads you to the counselor for you. I am not talking about someone who will just listen to you and 15 minutes before your hour session ends the counselor wraps up to schedule your next appointment. I pray you find a Christian counselor who listens, gives tools you can use, and cares enough to check in, assess, and follow-through with strategies to help you keep driving through the storm.

If you pull over and stop while the storm is

going on, the storm will soon completely cover you and always be just ahead of you. Your goal is to get through the storm to recovery. If you can afford a counselor and need it, put a bookmark here and pause reading to make the call to the one God leads you.

> Your goal is to get through the storm to recovery.

Every Christian needs a spiritual leader. Where I am from, if something happens, the female calls the pastor. The type of pastor who we consider good are those who immediately pray for our situation and show up at the hospital, home, court, or wherever we tell them. You should have a Spiritual Leader who is following the Bible and who you know takes caring for his flock seriously. Be careful not to expect your needs and emergencies to become the spiritual leader's priority. That person has a family who should be regarded respectfully.

> Spiritual Leader
>
> Every Christian needs a spiritual leader.

The church I joined after leaving the one for which my ex remains is a large church. I had no desire to be a member of a large congregation and to get lost in its numbers. Yet, the pastor of this church acts as if he has a small membership. He and his wife care, show concern, and support the membership at-large as if there are only one or two members. And, a highlight for me from my experience with my ex is that my pastor strives to live the Word of The Lord that he teaches; is the husband of one wife; and has no out-of-wedlock children. God has blessed the church to do and receive great things under their leadership even during the pandemic.

The Road to Recovery/Rebuilding

It may take months, or it may take years. Yet, the storm will not last always. There comes a time for recovery. You'll begin to see the clouds clear and the sun peeking. The key thing is to get the lessons that were intended and move on. Time waits for no one. There's no pause button for time. You may stop briefly, but time won't. Pray continually. Gather yourself and things. Thank God for Who He is and what He has done and is doing. Look forward and start moving right along.

> The key thing is to get the lessons that were intended and move on.

The Storm Continues...

Divorce Awarded

On March 2, 2020, my divorce was awarded on the grounds of adultery! It was the only day of the divorce process that I celebrated. This is one part of the storm that the scriptures were awakened to me. The Bible says it's best to celebrate the end of a thing than the beginning of a thing.

I put on an air, but I could not really celebrate the beginning of my marriage. On my first day as a wife, I learned my marriage was starting on a lie. I chose pride over the way of escape God gave me. That was a lesson about red flags. I now know when a red flag is confirmed, I better see that as my way of escape and run. On the day that my marriage had legally ended, I could celebrate the end of a marriage after 25 years and ten months. It wasn't what I wanted in the beginning nor was it my goal to devalue myself to prevent its ending.

Yet, God showed me that I wanted security, status, and financial things at the price of peace. I learned all of those are things that I should trust God for and what He continues to provide me. Money can buy you a bed, but it cannot buy you sleep. Money can buy you a wedding, but it cannot buy a marriage. It can buy you a house, but it cannot buy you a home. It can buy you medicine, but it cannot buy you good health. Because of God even with a new status of divorced, I am "Just Fine."

Acknowledge the Disappointment and Grieve the Process

Like Nike says, Just Do It. You cannot correct what you refuse to acknowledge. In the end, you will be "Just Fine" too. Don't delay the time by suppressing and ignoring feelings. Otherwise, they will rear their ugly heads when you least expect them. And, they'll delay the recovery process for you.

> You cannot correct what you refuse to acknowledge.

Healing

I don't know when mine happened, nor will you. But, healing will take place. I guarantee if you follow the Lord's leading to go through your storm, He will heal and restore you.

In case I didn't say it before, you can be angry. But sin not. Sinning only adds extra steps like: asking for forgiveness, being Godly sorrowful, and turning from the sin.

The Storm Continues...

Ask God for forgiveness for your roles in the storm. Don't act like you are without any. We all have some. I bet you didn't have any problems seeing some of mine just by reading this book. Your role may have been some act of commission and omission. Forgiveness is needed for thoughts, deeds, and inactive roles. Skipping this process, your prayers will be hindered. (I have had to forgive folks who don't even know or care that I know their involvement in my ex's adultery and schemes. The hardest to forgive are those who have taken a seat at my tables.) I know you want every one of your prayers answered. I know I do. Hint, hint: You would hate to delay the mate who God has for you in His timing.

> Ask for forgiveness for your roles in the storm. Don't act like you are without any. We all have some.

Trusting God

Nothing else needs to be said. Simply, T-R-U-S-T G-O-D!

NOTES

What Have or Are You Gleaning from Your Current or Previous Relationship "Coming out of The Storm?"_____

The Storm Continues ...

No matter whether one rebuilds, relocates, or gets buried alive, the next storm is on the horizon.

The Storm Cycle Continues – Headed to A Storm, In A Storm, Coming Out of A Storm

Calm

After the last storm which led to my divorce, I was doing well financially. By that I mean I had sufficient reoccurring income to cover my reoccurring, short term, and long term debt. I developed immeasurable comfort about my singleness. Unbelievably, the peace that Jesus left with me grew. It manifested shortly after I purchased and relocated into my "after the divorce" house. It truly feels like Home Sweet Home in my peaceful place!

In the Storm

Yep, you are correct. My calm period didn't last a full year following my divorce before the next storm hit. As with weather, it is true for everyday life. Storms may come one day after the other, within a span of weeks,

---
Storms may come one day after the other, within a span of weeks, and more than a month later.
---

and more than a month later. Regardless, the next storm is on the way.

I loss the job I acquired before the divorce was filed eight months after my divorce was awarded. Two months after I started a temporary job, it ended too. Both jobs ended during the nation's pandemic. I don't have enough funds coming in to cover my living expenses. At my age after having worked in the highest level and earning good pay, finding a new job with adequate pay is far from easy.

You might think I came out real pretty from the divorce since it was awarded based on adultery. It all depends on perspective and knowledge. At this point and four lawyers later, rest assured there remains many challenges, to say the least. I could list example-after-example. None of it really matters. And, some are none of my business. Fortunately, The Lord knows what I need and the desires of my heart. Every time He makes a way right-on-time!

What a welcomed day it will be when cooperation and amicable communication take place with my ex. Far too long, blatant and behind the scenes attempts to inconvenience and make life

The Storm Continues...

difficult for me have taken place. That will be book worthy but most importantly good for our son to see. What a blessing it will be for all to see the power of God working. (Please rest assured this has nothing to do with reuniting!)

So, there you have it. What appeared in my life as a storm yielded the life my ex wanted. The storm included blessings. Initially, I couldn't see them. I was too focused on what I wanted. I didn't know to expect what I received. I am smiling, know my value, making myself happy and accepting of my singleness. If my restoration includes a new and right relationship, I pray I am in the right position and obedient to God's leading.

> The storm included blessings.

Our teenage son continues to get to, through, and out of storms. Sometimes the brunt of his storms feels brutal, but it keeps me praying. I know he is trying his best to find his way and to fit in. This to him can be compounded by a need to balance his love for both parents who now live separately. He will realize he can have a love specifically for his father and a love specifically for his mother that gets demonstrated differently.

Fortunately, before this storm hit, I had worked to replenish my emergency preparedness kit. In it, there's plenty of love, grace, mercy, goodness, joy, faithfulness, and kindness. The area I tend to fall below half full is gratefulness. That bad thing called pride stands up because it feels entitled to access the former, finer lifestyle and things I was instrumental in creating. Then, I look around and realize how much more blessed and at peace I am.

> In it, there's plenty of love, grace, mercy, goodness, joy, faithfulness, and kindness.

I will continue to fill my stormy weather preparedness kit by reading my Bible and praying, praising, and trusting God to be my covering daily. It there are days that I feel like there's nothing in my kit, I will expect God to do like He has done in the past. He'll have His Holy Spirit to remind me or have someone contact me with a scripture or something else that encourages me to keep going.

Coming Out of the Storm ...

As I completed this book, I had to realize this book is like a movie that has no ending. For certainly, The Storm Continues...

Striving to drive through this current storm that can feel overwhelming because of my unemployment status, I continue to trust and pray I come out of this storm restored and whole with adequate finances. Ways I am trying to ensure this is by seeking new employment and continuing the work to develop my brand, body, and business. I acquired additional certifications to continue self-development and marketability. In addition to continuing education to maintain certifications in the Human Resource Management field, I have become certified as a life coach through Tony Gaskins Academy. And, I also renewed my Notary Public commission and have become certified as a Signing Agent to conduct mobile notary and closings for Home loans, refinances, home equity lines of credit, reverse mortgages, etc. All of this work can be conducted under the umbrella of my new business, Stacy Cobbins Consulting and Coaching, LLC.

NOTES

What Have or Are You Gleaning from Your Current or Previous Relationship as the "The Storm Continues?"

About the Author

Stacy L. Cobbins is the founding consultant and life coach at Stacy Cobbins Consulting and Coaching, LLC where she utilizes her education and experience in Human Resource Management, Accounting, and Life Coaching to assist individuals and businesses. Using self-discipline that pre-dates her eight years of military service in the United States Army Reserve, Stacy has established and worked other businesses for herself and others while working for private and public sector employers. Stacy turned a hobby for decorating sweet treats into a non-profit organization, Cups w/Caring Cakes. The charity's mission is to add smiles to the faces of those sick, abused, abandoned, and bereaved who receive her custom decorated sweet treats.

Stacy is the mother of one son, Preston "Cordell."

Stacy's heart desire is to live a life that is pleasing to her Lord and Savior, Jesus Christ. She enjoys cooking and planning and participating in fun.

Stacy L. Cobbins

The Storm Continues...